GCSE in a week

English

**Zoe Keeling and Cherie Rowe,
Abbey Tutorial College**

Where to find the information you need

The authors and publisher are grateful to the following for permission to reproduce copyright material: page 17 text © Express Newspapers, photographs © Torbay News Agency; page 50 © Richard Hillary courtesy of Jonathan Lovat Dickson and A M Heath & Co Ltd.; page 59 © The estate of John Steinbeck, William Heinemann; page 66 © Laurie Lee 1969, reproduced by permission of Penguin Books; page 77 © The estate of Wilfred Owen, the Collected Poems of Wilfred Owen edited by C Day Lewis, Chatto & Windus; page 84 © The estate of James Joyce, The Wylie Agency.

Letts Educational
Aldine Place
London W12 8AW
Tel: 0181 740 2266
Fax: 0181 743 8451
e-mail: mail@lettsed.co.uk
website: http://www.lettsed.co.uk

First published 1998
Reprinted 1998

Text © Zoe Keeling and Cherie Rowe 1998
Design and illustration © BPP (Letts Educational) Ltd 1998

British Library Cataloguing in Publication Data
A CIP record for this book is available from the British Library.

ISBN 1 85758 6972

Editorial, design and production by Hart McLeod, Cambridge

Printed in Great Britain by Sterling Press, Wellingborough NN8 6UF

Letts Educational is the trading name of BPP (Letts Educational) Ltd

Grammar, punctuation and spelling

Test your knowledge

10 minutes

1 Fill in the following gaps:

The verb in a sentence tells you what type of _____ took place and its form must agree with the _____ that performed it. The form of the verb also tells you when the action took place and, therefore, must be written in the correct _____ .

2 Circle the **incorrect** punctuation marks in the following sentences:

The postman, had been worried about delivering letters to the Jones' household all day. Since the arrival of their new dog. A once pleasant job had turned into a nightmare? Despite many complaint's to the family nothing had been done, to secure the dog.

3 Insert apostrophes appropriately in the following text:

It wasnt that the postman didnt like dogs, but Sparty wouldnt even give him a chance to get to know her. The dogs vicious attempts to savage him meant that the postmans job was becoming one of the worst Ive ever heard of.

4 Fill in the gaps in the following statements:

There are _____ letters in the alphabet known as vowels. These are _____ . All the other letters are called _____ . The way that a word is spelt sometimes depends on the length of the vowel which can either be long or _____ .

If you got them all right, skip to page 4

1

Grammar, punctuation and spelling

Improve your knowledge

20 minutes

1 Verbs are essential to sentences (the subjects and objects need something to do!) You will need to be careful to change their form to tell your reader:

What **kind** of action is being done: 'The package was **shaken**' (to shake)

Who performs the action: '**Jane shakes** the package' (singular)

 '**They shake** the package' (plural)

When the action was done (**tense**): 'She **shook** the package' (past)

 'She **shakes** the package' (present)

 'She **will shake** the package' (future)

2 Using correct punctuation in a sentence also helps to make your meaning clear to the reader. When you are writing, imagine that your script is going to be read out loud. A comma should be used to separate parts of a sentence with a short pause. A full stop is used at the end of every sentence for a longer pause where the meaning of the statement is complete. Remember that you can replace full stops with:

a) **!** if the sentence is an exclamation: 'What a scary dog**!**'

b) **?** if the sentence is a question: 'Is the dog scary**?**'

3 You will need to know where and when to insert apostrophes. They are used to:

a) Replace a missing letter or letters when two words are combined. The apostrophe should occupy the place left by the missing letter or letters, eg. didn't (did not); let's (let us).

b) Show that somebody owns something. The apostrophe is inserted after the word and before an added 's', eg. Peter's dog (the dog belonging to Peter).

  If the word is plural, and therefore already has an 's' at the end, the apostrophe should be placed after that 's', eg. the soldiers' dog (the dog belonging to the soldiers).

4 There are five letters in the alphabet which are called **vowels**. These are A, E, I, O and U. All the rest are known as **consonants**. Vowels can have a short sound (c**a**t, p**e**t, b**i**n, st**o**p, c**u**t) or a long sound (cr**a**te, m**e**ter, st**i**le, p**o**ke, d**u**ke). In certain words, the sound of the vowel gives a guide to its spelling:

a) after a short vowel sound you should double the consonant in the word, eg. pop, popping

b) an 'e' at the end of a word often lengthens the sound of the vowel before it, eg. pop, pope.

✓ *Now learn how to use this knowledge*

Grammar, punctuation and spelling

Use your knowledge

20 minutes

1 Choose the correct word in these sentences and underline it:

Hint 1

a) The postman and the dog is/are never going to be friends.
b) Tomorrow was/is/will be the last day that the postman delivers letters.
c) Everybody do/does their own job to the best of their ability.
d) If Sparty improved/improves her behaviour soon, maybe the postman will came/come back.

2 Insert full stops and commas in the appropriate places in the following text:

Hint 2

A dog which is a four-legged animal has many breeds although they can be affectionate there are wild dogs as well as domesticated they usually have big canine teeth excellent hearing powerful muscles and the ability to howl and bark other descriptive uses of the word refer to a stiff white collar that fastens at the back worn by clergymen and a fish that is like a small shark being in the dog house means that you are in disgrace whilst dog days are the hottest part of the year

3 Insert apostrophes in the following text:

Hint 3

The postmen at the sorting office werent too happy about the dogs behaviour. They thought that the familys decision to ignore the complaints wasnt acceptable and that this sort of thing shouldnt happen in such a good neighbourhood. The postmens next step was to tackle the family and their gruesome dog.

4

4 Give the plurals of the following words:

Hint 4

      crash   table   dairy   ditch   roof   knife   glass

5 Fill in the gaps in each sentence using the words in brackets:

Hint 5

Sparty ate the _____ (can/cane) of dog food.

The food was made from _____ (trip/tripe).

The family thought she looked _____ (cut/cute) and gave her a _____ (hug/huge) _____ (hug/huge).

6 Fill each blank with one of the words supplied after it in brackets:

Hint 6

The postman hadn't _____ (past/passed) the house for a long time. In the _____ (past/passed) he would have popped in for a cup of tea. The family _____ (new/knew) why he didn't speak to them. There was nothing _____ (new/knew) about this problem. Once the postman had gone, the dog was _____ (quiet/quite) and hardly ever barked. It was _____ (quiet/quite) a shame that it all ended like that. The family didn't know _____ (whether/weather) they should try to apologise.

Grammar, punctuation and spelling

Hints

1 When you are writing, try to keep all your verbs in the same tense. The past tense is the easiest.

2 Full stops should also be inserted after abbreviations and shortened words and phrases such as eg. and etc. Commas are also used to separate the parts of a list (eg. "carrots, peas, leeks and potatoes") and can be used like brackets in a sentence (eg. "The dog, who was very angry, bit the postman's ankle.")

3 "Its" should only have an apostrophe when it combines the two words "it" and "is", eg. "it's a nice day". An apostrophe should never be used with "its" to show possession. Also, when an apostrophe is used to combine negative words, eg. should not, it should always be placed between the "n" and the "t", eg. shouldn't.

4 Some words are always used in the plural, eg. trousers, scissors. Other words stay the same when plural, eg. sheep, deer.

5 If you find spelling difficult, try to look for the simple words which are contained within a longer word, eg. dis/agree/able. If a couple of words are particularly difficult, try using the letters as the first letters of words to make a memorable sentence, eg. debt: **D**on't **E**ver **B**orrow **T**enners! In an exam, if you come to write a word which you are doubtful about spelling, try to choose another word with the closest meaning that you know you can spell.

6 Always re-read your work to check that the spelling, punctuation and grammar are accurate.

Grammar, punctuation and spelling

Answers

1 a) are   b) will be   c) does   d) improves, come.

2 A dog, which is a four-legged animal, has many breeds. Although they can be affectionate, there are wild dogs as well as domesticated. They usually have big canine teeth, excellent hearing, powerful muscles and the ability to howl and bark. Other descriptive uses of the word refer to a stiff white collar that fastens at the back, worn by clergymen, and a fish that is like a small shark. Being in the dog house means that you are in disgrace, whilst dog days are the hottest part of the year.

3 The postmen at the sorting office weren't too happy about the dog's behaviour. They thought that the family's decision to ignore the complaints wasn't acceptable and that this sort of thing shouldn't happen in such a good neighbourhood. The postmen's next step was to tackle the family and their gruesome dog.

4 crashes, tables, dairies, ditches, roofs, knives, glasses.

5 can, tripe, cute, huge, hug.

6 passed, past, knew, new, quiet, quite, whether.

Essay skills

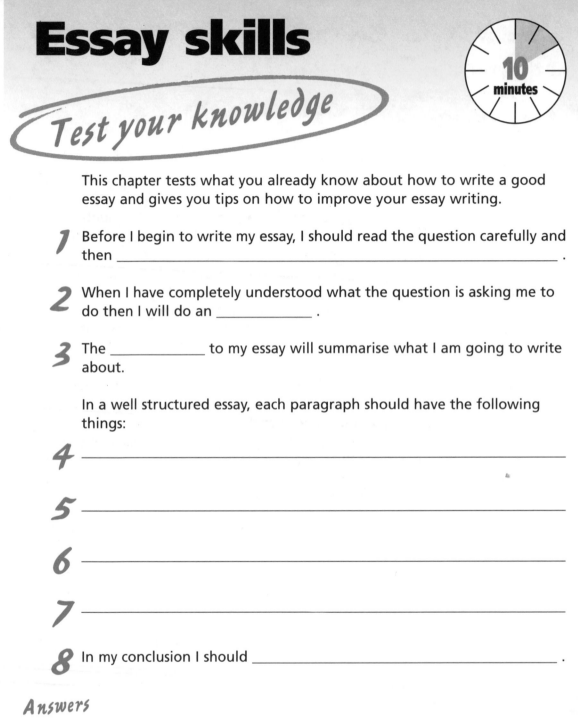

Test your knowledge

10 minutes

This chapter tests what you already know about how to write a good essay and gives you tips on how to improve your essay writing.

1 Before I begin to write my essay, I should read the question carefully and then _____ .

2 When I have completely understood what the question is asking me to do then I will do an _____ .

3 The _____ to my essay will summarise what I am going to write about.

In a well structured essay, each paragraph should have the following things:

4 _____

5 _____

6 _____

7 _____

8 In my conclusion I should _____ .

8

Essay skills
Improve your knowledge

20 minutes

1 Examiners want you to organise your ideas in a logical order. When you achieve this you will get extra marks for your essay writing. Remember to plan what you will want to say and to allow yourself a little time to think about this carefully. The content of your essay will read so much better.

Always think carefully about what the question is asking you to do. If you take out the important parts and jot them down, you can be sure that you are answering all of the question, and not just some of it. This helps to get your brain into gear and gives you confidence because you know exactly what you are supposed to be doing.

eg. **Discuss the arguments for and against fox hunting.**

a   b   c

a) Consider the points.

b) What are the points in favour?

c) What are the points against?

2 An essay plan ensures that your essay is well constructed. It is the ideal way to make sure that you think before you write. It's like thinking about what you will be wearing to the job interview the night before. If you plan your essay, you can make sure you answer all of the question and get the maximum marks.

Planning your essay

Make brief notes according to the following headings:

3 Introduction

In your introduction always try to use some of the key words from the question. In this way you can make sure that you are answering the question and not waffling. It also helps because the most difficult thing in an examination is actually writing the first sentence. Planning and using the words from the question should make this much easier for you.

eg. You could start with the question: Is fox hunting a sport or is it animal cruelty?

Here, you would be using both sides of the argument to introduce your essay.

4 Key points

A key point is a main idea or point that is relevant to the question. In an essay, try to have about five key points.

An example of your plan might be:

Key point 1. Argument for fox hunting: tradition
Key point 2. Argument for fox hunting: keeps people employed
Key point 3. Argument for and against: people disagree because it is an emotional subject
Key point 4. Argument against: cruel to the fox
Key point 5. Argument against: cruel to the hounds.

One good way (of many) to begin a paragraph is to use phrases like: I think, I consider, I thought, I believe or My view is. These are all different ways of expressing your opinion and they improve your use of English and how you make your arguments.

5 Illustrating your point

An examiner wants to know why you think something is the case. When you illustrate a key point, you are showing the examiner how well you understand what you have read.

eg. Key point 1 could be illustrated by writing that tradition is important for the village community and for historical reasons.

You could also use a quotation or close reference to the source material.

6 Commenting on the language used

If you are writing an essay in response to something you have read then show how the writer uses the language.

eg. You might write: "The way the two opposing parties talk about fox hunting is different. The huntsman used the term 'fox hunting' and the animal rights spokesman used 'blood-sports'. The latter definition has a more shocking impact on the reader."

Explaining the effect of the words used shows the examiner that you understand and realise the importance of how writers use language for specific effects.

7 Linking sentence to the next paragraph

Keep all of your ideas in one chain. Think about each paragraph as a link in the chain. Always read over what you have written before you end your paragraph and start your new one. Forward planning makes your essay writing more effective.

eg. To link the key point that fox hunting is cruel and the key point that it is cruel to the hounds, you might write:

"However, the fox is not the only animal to suffer."

8 Conclusion

This is important and you should always aim to finish your essay and leave the examiner with a lasting good impression of your skills. You can do this by using similar words to those in the question.

Read through the key points of your essay to provide you with a summary of your response. This is also a good place to explain how you responded to the question. For example:

"Although I can appreciate that people use the argument that fox hunting has been an English tradition for years, I think that some traditions need to be changed. It was traditional to burn people because they were thought to be witches but we no longer carry out that practice. I believe that it takes courage and persistence to change traditions but the end result is worth it. Foxes do not deserve to suffer because of tradition and therefore I am against fox hunting."

Now learn how to use this knowledge

Essay skills

Use your knowledge

20 minutes

1 Provide an essay plan for the following question:

Discuss the arguments for and against using animals in research.

Hint 1

Question Breakdown:

_____

2 Introduction:

Hint 2

_____

3 Key point 1:

Hint 3

_____

4 Key point 2:

Hint 4

_____

5 Key point 3:

Hint 5

_____

6 Key point 4:

Hint 6

_____

7 Key point 5:

Hint 7

_____

8 Conclusion:

Hint 8

_____

✓ *Hints and answers follow*

Essay skills

Hints

1 Think about what the question is asking you to do. Make sure you consider all the parts of the question before you begin to write.

2 Think about how you are going to tackle the question in your essay and tell your reader what it is you are going to write about.

3 to 7 These are five key ideas – but there could be more or fewer. Each idea should make a significant contribution to your essay. Try to make your key points interesting to the reader. Think about an example where it might be acceptable to use animals for testing. Are there any alternatives to this point? In key point 7, try to weigh up the reasons for and against testing.

8 A conclusion should be a brief summary of your essay. Remember to use the words 'for' and 'against' which are in the question. Try to leave the examiner with a clear understanding of your opinion.

Essay skills

Answers

Remember that these are only a few suggested answers; you will certainly have other, different ideas! The important thing is to structure your ideas logically and clearly.

1 Discuss and consider:
Arguments for: when could testing on animals be acceptable?
Arguments against: when is testing on animals unacceptable?

2 Vivisection is a topic people feel strongly about. Some support it for medical or scientific reasons, others are against it for cultural or humane reasons.

3 Argument for: medical – finding cures for life-threatening diseases.

4 Argument against: medical – we can use alternative tests such as those on synthetic cells or tissues.

5 Argument for: research – to improve our own standards of living, provide little luxuries.

6 Argument against: cosmetics – plenty of manufacturers do not need to use animals to test their products.

7 Argument for/against – it is an individual's decision whether to buy products or not but medical research has saved lives.

8 Conclusion: my view is that vivisection is justifiable in certain situations because it saves lives. However, if there are alternative ways to test new drugs and cures then I think we should use them.

Reading newspaper articles

Test your knowledge

10 minutes

Newspaper articles are usually written in a distinctive narrative style. The more familiar you are with newspaper styles, the better prepared you'll be for these questions, so read as broadly as you can whenever you can.

1 The **purpose** of a newspaper article is to provide _____ for the reader about a recent news event.

2 Fill in the gaps below to describe the **structure** of a newspaper article:

A newspaper article has a title called a a) _____ at the top and may be sectioned throughout the rest of the text with smaller b) _____ . The text is laid out in c) _____ and a summary of the story is found in the d) _____ paragraph.

3 Writers need to support or prove their statements with some form of _____ .

4 Writers (or journalists) can assert their own opinions in an article by using _____ language.

5 The **register** of a newspaper article can either be informal or _____ .

6 Informal newspapers, such as *The Sun*, are known as _____ papers.

15

Reading newspaper articles

20 minutes

1 The purpose of a newspaper article is to give a reader the **facts** about a recent news story as concisely and accurately as possible.

2 A newspaper article will have a **headline** at the top which uses some aspect of the story in an interesting way: this catches your attention. Subheadings indicate what each section of the story is about. The text is written in columns and the first paragraph briefly summarises the whole story.

3 To add realism, and to support their story, writers often directly **quote** or **summarise** what people have said. These people may be involved in the story or may be experts on the subject matter of the story.

4 Although a newspaper article gives the reader information, writers can use language to present facts in a **biased** way. This means that – often subtly – they show their own opinion. You will need to look closely at the meaning of the words so that you can 'read between the lines'.

5 **Register**, or tone, is important for establishing how the writer wants you to react to the article. A formal register makes the article serious while an informal (colloquial) register is more relaxed and friendly. Remember that an informal register will contain abbreviations and non-standard phrases (see chapter on Reading adverts, page 30, point 3).

6 Newspapers that have an informal register such as *The Sun*, *The Mirror* and *The Express*, are called **tabloid** papers. These generally present stories in a less serious way and use more casual language than newspapers like *The Times* or *The Daily Telegraph*.

✔ *Now learn how to use this knowledge*

Reading newspaper articles

Use your knowledge

20 minutes

1 Using the following article about the results of a visit to a dentist, label a) – d) correctly to identify the structure of the article.

---

20 NEWS THE EXPRESS ON TUESDAY JULY 8 1997

Revenge on the dentist

Pub landlord attacked him, court told

WHEN DENTIST Grahame Mason went for a pub lunch he was painfully extracted from the premises.

Landlord Peter Malkin (below), 58, a former patient, got revenge on the 16-stone surgeon for the discomfort of previous dental work by throwing a pint of beer in his face and dumping him outside.

Their confrontation at the bar in the Churston Court Hotel was the result of bad feeling between the two, a court heard yesterday. It led to the licensee being accused of assault. Paul Green, prosecuting, said Mr Mason had

EXPRESS REPORTER

just ordered a pint at the bar when the licensee marched over and started a dispute, complaining about dental work a year earlier.

"Mr Mason's wife Janine heard them arguing and didn't want it to spoil their outing, so she went over and asked them to stop," Mr Green said.

"Malkin became increasingly annoyed and picked up the full pint of beer Mr Mason had just ordered. Then he threw the contents into Mr Mason's face, soaking him, his hair and clothes, and also drenching Mrs Mason, who was standing at his shoulder."

Mr Mason asked the barmaid to call the police but she ignored him, he added.

The licensee then tried to eject the dentist by picking him up, but couldn't lift him, Torbay magistrates were told.

Malkin called two members of staff to help physically eject him and together they carried Mr Mason out and dumped him on the ground.

In a scuffle outside, Mr Mason (below) was kicked in the ribs as he lay on the ground, Mr Green said.

When he got up, Malkin pushed him and he fell backwards, hitting his head.

Malkin, of Brixham, Devon, denies assault, damaging Mr Mason's car, and assaulting his brother-in-law, Roger Prior, who tried to intervene.

---

a) _____

b) _____

c) _____

d) _____

2 Read the article carefully and then answer the following questions:

a) Using your own words, summarise in about 200 – 250 words exactly what happened in the Churston Court Hotel pub. *Hint 1*

_____

_____

_____

_____

_____

_____

_____

_____

_____

_____

_____

_____

_____

_____

_____

_____

b) What sort of evidence or facts does the writer use to show the reader what happened? *Hint 2*

_____

_____

_____

_____

_____

c) Is the article written in a formal or informal register?
Identify two examples of words or phrases which helped you make your decision.

Hint 3

_____

_____

_____

_____

_____

d) How are the two men named? How are the females named?

Hint 4

_____

_____

_____

_____

e) Pick out all the words that describe Mr Malkin's actions.
Are they positive or negative words?

Hint 5

_____

_____

_____

_____

_____

_____

Hints and answers follow

Reading newspaper articles

1 When you summarise the contents of a newspaper article, you must use **your own words**. Pick out the important facts of the story and then write your answer using the closest words in meaning you can think of to those used in the text (looking through a thesaurus might help). Remember, try to stick to the word limit.

2 The writer has used Mr Green's words to provide the facts of the story, which makes the story biased in Mr Mason's favour. Therefore, by choosing to quote from Mr Mason's lawyer, the writer has shown bias in the story.

3 An informal register is used here to present the story in a light-hearted and humorous way.

4 The writer shows a humorous attitude towards both men, by labelling them using their personal attributes. Mr Mason's weight is mentioned, as is Mr Malkin's age. Both men are labelled by their professions and the relationship between the two is established through Mr Malkin being named as "a former patient".

5 The writer again shows a positive bias towards Mr Mason. Throughout the text he is given the title "Mr", whilst Mr Malkin is denied his title and is simply named "Malkin". This means that we feel less respect for Mr Malkin.

   Being named by a first name only may command even less respect. Mr Mason's wife is named as "Janine".

   The writer's bias is also shown by the words chosen to describe the two men. Words associated with Mr Malkin are either violent or negative. The photo supports this! Words associated with Mr Mason and his wife are, by contrast, passive.

Reading newspaper articles

Answers

1 a) columns, b) first paragraph, c) subheading, d) headline.

2 a) When dentist Grahame Mason ordered a pint in the Churston
      Court Hotel, a previous patient and Pub Landlord, Peter Malkin,
      complained about his dental work of a year ago. Mrs Mason
      tried to stop the argument, but Peter Malkin threw a pint of
      beer over Grahame Mason whilst the barmaid ignored Mrs
      Mason's requests that she should call the police. The landlord
      attempted to physically remove Mr Mason himself, but had to
      get help from two members of his staff. They carried him
      outside and Mr Mason claims that he was kicked in the ribs and
      pushed backwards so that he hit his head. Mr Malkin now faces
      an assault charge.

   b) The writer uses direct quotations from Mr Green, the
      prosecutor, and summarises what evidence the court had
      heard.

   c) An informal register. Abbreviations are used, such as
      "couldn't", as are standard phrases such as "marched over"
      and "day out". Words that are colloquial include "dumping"
      and "scuffle".

   d) Mr Mason is named as: "Dentist Grahame Mason",
      "16-stone surgeon" and "Mr Mason".

      Mr Malkin is named as: "Pub landlord", "Landlord Peter
      Malkin, 58", "a former patient", "the licensee" and "Malkin".

      Mrs Mason is named as: "Janine" and "Mrs Mason".

   e) Words associated with Mr Malkin include: "revenge",
      "dispute", "complained", "annoyed", "drenched", "soaked",
      "eject" (repeated twice), "dumped" (repeated twice),
      "kicked", "pushed", "damaging" and "assaulting". They are
      violent or negative words.

Writing newspaper articles

Test your knowledge

10 minutes

1 Fill in the gaps with the correct words:

The title of a newspaper article is called a _____ and should attract the reader towards the story. The number of words in this title should normally be no more than _____ .

2 Tick the correct answer. A subheading is:

a) A very large, prominent title found at the top of the front page of a newspaper. ❑

b) A small title that sections off parts of the text within a newspaper article. ❑

c) A sentence which is inserted at the bottom of a newspaper article when a reporter has forgotten to include it in the text. ❑

3 When the text on a printed page is sectioned into narrow bars running from top to bottom, the strips of text are called _____ .

4 Which section of a newspaper article contains a summary of the whole story? _____ .

5 Tick which level of formality you would use to write about the following topics:

	Formal	Informal
a) The third robbery of a jewellery shop in two weeks.	❑	❑
b) A record number of puppies born in a dog's litter.	❑	❑
c) Two people get married in a supermarket.	❑	❑
d) An air plane crash in a European country.	❑	❑

✔ *If you got them all right, skip to page 24*

Writing newspaper articles

Improve your knowledge

20 minutes

1. A newspaper article must have a **headline** which is relevant to the story. Try to make it interesting since the headline should capture your reader's attention. The headline should be no more than ten words long, but you can leave out small words like "a" and "the" as long as the meaning is still clear, eg. "Two men save a deer" can be written as "Two men save deer".

2. It's a good idea to include **subheadings** in the text. These act like small titles and give some indication of what each section is about.

3. Newspaper articles are set out in **columns** rather than long paragraphs.

4. In the **first** paragraph you should briefly summarise the whole story. The rest of the text gives details of the event.

5. The level of formality will depend on which newspaper you are writing for. Remember that tabloids, like *The Sun*, *The Mirror* and local papers, tend to use **informal** registers whilst the nationals, like *The Times* and *The Daily Telegraph*, use a **formal** register. The level of formality also depends on the subject matter. A humorous story needs a colloquial register; a serious story needs a higher level of formality.

✔ *Now learn how to use this knowledge*

Writing newspaper articles

As part of your exam, your knowledge of newspaper article styles might be tested by a question which asks you to write your own. Try this for practice.

1 Read the following facts carefully:

- A local lottery sum of £5,000 has been won.

  Hint 1

- The winner is a fifteen year old student from Croydon who is studying for his GCSE exams.

  Hint 2

- Because he is under eighteen, he has been told that he cannot be given his winnings.

  Hint 3

- His name is Tim Williams and he likes football. He was hoping to spend the money on a trip abroad to support his local team.

  Hint 4

- He bought the ticket from a newsagent's in Streatham. The owner's name is Simon Thorpe. He has two children. He has said, "I didn't realise when I sold the ticket to Tim that he was underage. Children look so old these days that, to be honest, it didn't even cross my mind to ask if he was over eighteen or ask for ID. I get a lot of young people buying these lottery tickets and I think I will have very long queues in my shop if I try to check everyone's age. I don't think it's my fault. He should have known that he's not old enough to buy a ticket, but at the same time, I do feel sorry for him and I'm sure that he is very disappointed."

  Hint 5

- Tim Williams' mother has six children and she has lived in Croydon for 32 years. She has said, "My son bought that lottery ticket in good faith and he paid good money for it. I think that they just want to hold on to the money themselves, using any excuse that they can. Tim used his pocket money, which I gave him, to buy that ticket, so if anything, the lottery winnings belong to me."

  Hint 6

- A spokesman for the lottery, who would not give his name, has said, "We are sorry that Tim cannot be awarded his winnings, but the rules clearly state that lottery winners must be over eighteen. We cannot make exceptions to the rules and I'm afraid that Tim will have to be disappointed on this occasion. We have offered to make a financial contribution to the educational facilities of his school."

Using the above facts, write a brief article on this story for your local newspaper.

Hints and answers follow

Writing newspaper articles

Hints

1. The headline to this story needs to be eye-catching but also needs to give an indication of the story content. You could use exaggeration to attract your reader's attention, eg. "Underage gambler is denied winnings" or keep the headline more formal, "Underage student refused lottery win". The headline summarises the story in a few well chosen words.

2. Subheadings within the text should be kept short and should summarise the content of the different sections. This story demands that there must be sections on:

   a) The newsagent's reaction

   b) The mother's reaction

   c) The lottery spokesman's reaction.

   Try to think of one or two words which summarise the content of each section:

   a) Too busy to check/difficulty telling the age of customers

   b) Disgusted

   c) Rules are rules.

3. In the first paragraph, you must pick out the key facts so that you tell the story as concisely as possible, eg. "A fifteen year old lottery winner has been told that he cannot receive his £5,000 winnings because he is underage".

4. It will be important to establish who Tim Williams, his mother and the newsagent are and how you want to name them: "Tim Williams, a GCSE student from Croydon", "Mrs Williams, a mother of six" and "Mr Thorpe, who owns the newsagents in Streatham". It is as important to know what information to leave out because it is not relevant as it is to know what to include, eg. "Mrs Williams has lived in Croydon for 32 years" is not relevant to the story.

5 Quote sections of speech which best represent the participants' feelings and opinions. Don't quote everything that they say; your article will become too long and rambling. If you use a really long quote, the point often gets lost, eg. "I didn't realise when I sold the ticket to Tim that he was underage. Children look so old these days. I will have very long queues in my shop if I try to check everyone's age", said Mr Thorpe. Cut the quote down, so that you only include the key point that Mr Thorpe "didn't realise" that Tim was underage.

6 Since you have been asked to write for a local paper and the content of the story is not very serious, an informal register can be used.

Writing newspaper articles

Answers

6   There are lots of different ways to write the article using the information provided. This model includes the main features: can you identify them here and in your own article?

SCHOOLBOY LOTTERY LOSER

Local student Tim Williams, who is studying for his GCSEs next Summer, faced disappointment last night after a local lottery refused to pay out on his £5,000 winning ticket because, at fifteen, Tim is three years younger than the minimum age required to buy a lottery ticket. Tim had been planning to spend some of his winnings on a ticket to follow his local football team, Croydon F.C., for their qualifying match abroad next Wednesday night. He is very upset that his hopes have been dashed.

Shopkeeper made mistake

Tim bought his winning ticket from a newsagent in Streatham. Owner Simon Thorpe expressed his regret at the news saying, "I do feel sorry for him," but added that Tim should have known he was too young to buy a ticket. Thorpe, himself a father of two teenagers, said that it was increasingly hard to tell how old some of his young customers were. He told us, "Children look so old these days that, to be honest, it didn't even cross my mind to ask if he was over eighteen or ask for ID."

More complicated

Tim's mother, Mrs Williams, a mother of six, said that the ruling was unfair on her son because he "paid good money" for the ticket. She added that the case was not as simple as it seemed because "Tim used his pocket money, which I gave him, to buy that ticket, so if anything, the lottery winnings belong to me."

No exceptions to the rule

A spokesman for the lottery, who refused to be named, told us "the rules clearly state that lottery winners must be over eighteen". He added that the lottery had offered to make a financial contribution to the educational facilities at Tim's school as a way of compensating him.

Reading adverts

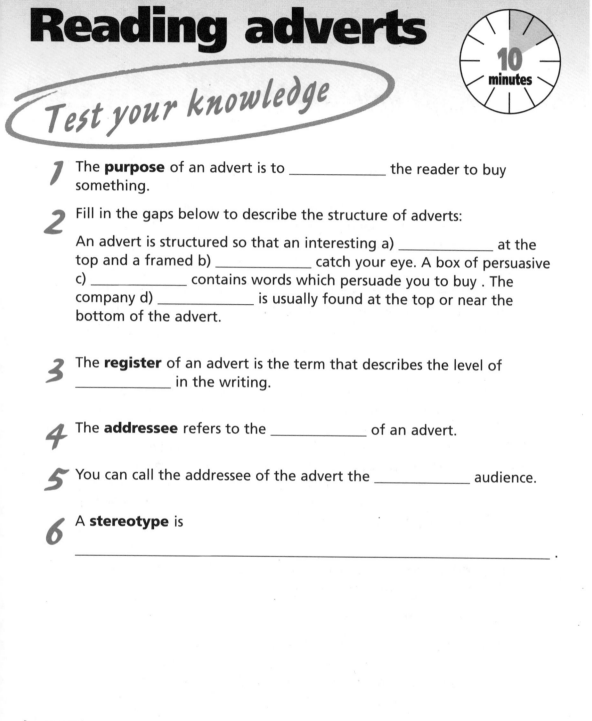

Test your knowledge

10 minutes

1 The **purpose** of an advert is to _____ the reader to buy something.

2 Fill in the gaps below to describe the structure of adverts:

An advert is structured so that an interesting a) _____ at the top and a framed b) _____ catch your eye. A box of persuasive c) _____ contains words which persuade you to buy . The company d) _____ is usually found at the top or near the bottom of the advert.

3 The **register** of an advert is the term that describes the level of _____ in the writing.

4 The **addressee** refers to the _____ of an advert.

5 You can call the addressee of the advert the _____ audience.

6 A **stereotype** is

_____ .

Answers

1 persuade **2** a) caption b) picture c) text d) logo **3** formality **4** reader **5** intended **6** the fixed ideas we have of the characteristics of people or certain sections of society

If you got them all right, skip to page 32

29

Reading adverts

Improve your knowledge

20 minutes

1 The **purpose** of an advert is to persuade you to buy either a product (goods you can take away with you, like perfume) or a service (where professionals do a job for you, like plumbing). Advertising is used when a seller wants to reach a really wide audience instead of trying to promote his or her product person to person.

2 Adverts usually have a **catchy title** or heading at the top, some form of picture (either an illustration or photograph), a persuasive piece of writing (the text) and the company slogan somewhere prominent on the page.

3 The **register** of an advert is the level of formality in the writing. When you chat with your friends, you talk in a casual way and when you speak with a stranger you use more formal language (in a nutshell, this is the difference between "yeah" and "yes"). You can call an informal register **colloquial.** A colloquial text will have abbreviations, eg. "isn't" instead of "is not", slang terms, eg. "copper" instead of police officer and standard phrases that are often used in casual English, eg. "He's the talk of the town".

4 The **addressee** of an advert is the person who reads the advert. Consider the following examples:

"**It** is possible to buy this car".   and   "**You** can buy this car".

In the second example, the reader is addressed as "you" so that the advert seems to speak directly to you as an individual. The advert becomes personal and you are supposed to forget that it is read by hundreds of people!

5 An advert will be aimed at a particular audience – those who are most likely to buy the product or use the service. You can call these groups of people the **intended audience.** For example, the intended audience of computer game adverts tends to be children, whereas the intended audience of hair dye adverts tends to be women. Once the advertiser decides upon the intended audience, the advert will be targeted to appeal to that audience.

6 **Stereotype** is the term used to describe the fixed ideas that we have about groups of people. We tend to think that men are strong, decisive and powerful whilst women are delicate, sensitive and caring. Of course, people don't really fit into strict groups like this, but advertisers use stereotypes to appeal to their intended audience. So, a car advert aimed at women might stress its safety, comfort and reliability, while a car advert aimed at men might stress its fast speed, technical advancement and aggressive image.

✔ *Now learn how to use this knowledge*

Reading adverts

Use your knowledge

20 minutes

1 Adverts are carefully constructed by advertisers, to make them as persuasive as possible to the reader. Look a little more closely at this one.

Label the boxes a) – d) correctly to identify the structure of the advert shown below:

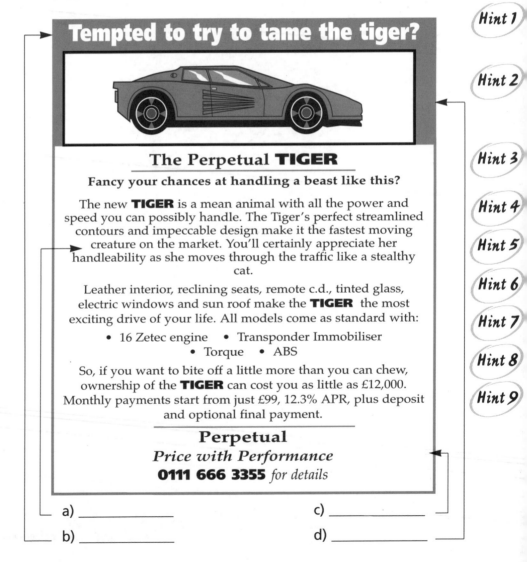

Tempted to try to tame the tiger?

The Perpetual **TIGER**

Fancy your chances at handling a beast like this?

The new **TIGER** is a mean animal with all the power and speed you can possibly handle. The Tiger's perfect streamlined contours and impeccable design make it the fastest moving creature on the market. You'll certainly appreciate her handleability as she moves through the traffic like a stealthy cat.

Leather interior, reclining seats, remote c.d., tinted glass, electric windows and sun roof make the **TIGER** the most exciting drive of your life. All models come as standard with:

- 16 Zetec engine • Transponder Immobiliser
- Torque • ABS

So, if you want to bite off a little more than you can chew, ownership of the **TIGER** can cost you as little as £12,000. Monthly payments start from just £99, 12.3% APR, plus deposit and optional final payment.

Perpetual
Price with Performance
0111 666 3355 *for details*

Hint 1

Hint 2

Hint 3

Hint 4

Hint 5

Hint 6

Hint 7

Hint 8

Hint 9

a) _____   c) _____

b) _____   d) _____

2 Try to find the following features, writing the appropriate letter next to the examples in the advert:

> A = Alliteration
> M = Metaphor
> S = Simile
> R = Repetition
> L = Listing
> T = Technical language
> P = Positive descriptive words.

3 Fill in the gaps:

The reader is addressed as a) _____ , making the advert personal. Casual phrases such as b) _____ and _____ and abbreviations like c) _____ make the register of the advert d) _____ .

Hint 10

Hint 11

Hint 12

Hints and answers follow

Reading adverts

Hints

Evaluate how effective the advert has been in persuading you to buy the car. Quote from the advert to illustrate each point you make. Consider:

1 **The caption:**

   a) Contains alliteration ("Tempted", "tame", "tiger") written in a large, interesting font, making the caption visually striking.

   b) Asks a question, capturing the reader's attention and luring him or her into reading the text to find the answer.

   c) Introduces the tiger metaphor (see "metaphor" below).

2 **The picture** draws the reader's attention to it because the car is attractive, sporty and red.

3 **The company logo** contains alliteration ("price" and "performance"), to make the company name memorable.

4 **A metaphor** is used throughout the text, comparing the car with a tiger ("beast", "mean animal", and "creature"), so that the tiger's power, speed and ferocity are associated with the car.

5 **A simile** is used to compare the car with a "stealthy cat", extending the tiger metaphor.

6 **Repetition.** The word "Tiger", mentioned six times, ensures that the name of the car sticks in the reader's mind.

7 **Lists.** Features such as "leather interior" and "reclining seats", made into a list, emphasise the sheer number of the car's good points.

8 **Technical language** makes the car sound ultra modern and desirable.

9 **Positive descriptive words.** There are a number of these ("perfect" and "exciting"), including the term "as **little** as £12,000", which tries to suggest a low cost for an amazing vehicle.

10 **Informal address**, using the term "you", makes the reader feel he or she is being addressed in a friendly, trustworthy way.

11 to 12 **Casual phrases.** These help to make the advert more friendly to the reader: the everyday language suggests that a person well known – and trusted – to them is telling them about the product and its advantages.

Reading adverts

Answers

1 a) text
   b) heading or caption
   c) company logo
   d) picture.

2 A = "**t**empted to **t**ry to **t**ame the **t**iger" or "**P**erpetual **p**rice with **p**erformance"

   M = tiger or big cat

   S = like a stealthy cat

   R = Tiger

   L = leather interior, reclining seats etc.

   T = 16 Zetec engine, Torque, Transponder Immobiliser, ABS

   P = "perfect", "impeccable", "exciting", "superior".

3 a) "you"
   b) "fancy your chances", "bite off a little more than you can chew"
   c) "You'll"
   d) colloquial or informal.

Writing adverts

Test your knowledge

1 Tick the correct answer. The caption of an advert is its:

a) humorous illustration or picture ❑

b) eye-catching title ❑

c) product for sale. ❑

2 Fill in the gaps:

An illustration or _____ in an advert attracts the reader by showing the product in an _____ way.

3 Tick the boxes to indicate whether the following phrases are formal or informal:

	Formal	Informal
a) Ben thought that he just couldn't get enough of it.	❑	❑
b) Mr Thomas decided that he would like some more.	❑	❑
c) It was like a red rag to a bull.	❑	❑
d) He became very angry.	❑	❑

4 Tick the correct answer. The addressee of an advert is:

a) The person who reads the advert. ❑

b) The person who writes the advert. ❑

c) The contact details of the company. ❑

5 Tick which of the following words you would consider using to describe a product in an advert:

adequate ❑   good ❑   satisfactory ❑   superb ❑

excellent ❑   poor ❑   fantastic ❑   perfect ❑

Answers

1 b) 2 picture, attractive 3 a) informal b) formal c) informal d) formal 4 a) 5 good, superb, excellent, fantastic, perfect

✓ If you got them all right, skip to page 39

Writing adverts

Improve your knowledge

20 minutes

1 A successful advert needs an interesting, eye-catching caption. Try using humour, alliteration or asking a question in the caption to attract the reader's attention.

2 Most adverts contain some form of picture or illustration. They may show the product itself, or else something appealing to attract the reader's attention. You should show where the picture should go and what the picture should be. Do not spend too much time drawing the illustrations in perfect detail; an outline will earn you just as many marks in the exam.

3 Choose appropriate language and register for your intended audience. For example, if you are writing for children, you need to keep the language simple and the register informal. You may wish to choose more advanced language and a formal register when your target audience is, for example, professional people.

4 Address the reader as "you". It makes the advert personal, as if you are writing to each individual.

5 An advert must sell its product, so you will need to list all the attractive features of the product or service. Use positive words, eg. "excellent", to describe the product, and make the key words stand out by repeating them in different parts of the text. You can also use imagery to describe the product. This makes the advert memorable and brings the description to life.

✔ *Now learn how to use this knowledge*

Writing adverts

Use your knowledge

20 minutes

1 You have been asked to write a leaflet to advertise a local youth club which is hoping to attract young teenagers to spend their spare time at the club. The advert will be placed in a local newspaper and you have been given the following information to help you write the advert:

- The youth club is called *The Oasis* and is open from 10 am until 10 pm on Saturdays.

- The club has five snooker tables, a variety of games machines, a football pitch, karting field, cafeteria and weekly disco.

- The club is open to anyone between the ages of fourteen and sixteen. The karting costs £4.00 per hour, but all other activities are free.

- An adult is present at the club at all times.

- Alcohol is not allowed in the club.

- The address and phone number of the club are:

  The Oasis,
  17 High Street,
  Mansfield,
  Staffs,
  ST13 3BU.
  Tel: 01911 112371

Hint 1

Hint 2

Hint 3

Hint 4

Hint 5

Hint 6

Hint 7

Hint 8

Hints and answers follow

Writing adverts

Hints

1   The caption for this advert needs to appeal to young people. Since the club provides activities and encourages young people to get together, questions which target boredom and loneliness might be suitable, eg. "Feeling bored on a Saturday?" Humour in the caption would show that the club is a place to have fun.

2   A picture should give the reader a visual idea of what the club is like. A picture of young people looking happy, chatting over a game of pool or at the disco suggests that you will have a good time, that you will make new friends and that both sexes are welcome.

3   The register of the advert should attract the desired audience. A colloquial, informal register is more approachable to teenagers than a formal style, so you should try to write as if you were speaking to the reader. Addressing the reader as "you" also helps.

4   Before you start writing, list all the positive words you can think of so you don't use them more than once.

5   Since most teenagers worry about the cost of activities, repeating the word "free" in this advert is useful, eg. free membership, free snooker and free disco.

6   You can also use bullet points to list all the attractive features of the club so that the reader can see how much is on offer:

- Five snooker tables
- Games machines
- Cafeteria
- Karting
- Football field
- Disco

7   You must decide what information to leave out of your advert. That an adult is present and that no alcohol is allowed at the club stress its safety. This is highly attractive to parents, but not so much to teenagers! Therefore, to make the advert appealing to the desired audience, it would be acceptable not to include these two facts.

8   You may want to introduce the address and phone number with a question encouraging the reader to get in touch, eg. "Why not give us a ring today on ... or drop in to see us all?"

Writing adverts

Answer

1 There are lots of different ways of writing your advert for the youth club, but you could check the following model against your own to make sure you've included everything.

> # There's nothing to do on Saturdays in Mansfield?
>
> YES THERE IS! Come to *The Oasis* youth club – membership's free and it's open between 10 in the morning and 10 at night every Saturday. Anyone between the ages of fourteen and sixteen is welcome, and there are loads of free activities on offer, including:
>
> - five snooker tables
> - games machines
> - football
> - cafe
> - night-time disco
>
> For a small charge, you can even have a go at karting.
>
> [perhaps add a picture here of young people enjoying themselves at the club]
>
> **Why not give us a ring today on Mansfield 112371, or drop in to meet us at:**
>
> **The Oasis, 17 High Street, Mansfield.**

Special reports

10 minutes

1 Fill in the boxes with the correct word:

When writing a letter to a friend, your address should be in the top
a) _____ hand corner of the page. The word b) _____
should be inserted before the person's name to start the letter.

2 Tick the boxes to indicate which farewells might be appropriate to end
a letter to a friend:

Yours sincerely	❑	Lots of love	❑	Yours faithfully	❑
Best wishes	❑	See you soon	❑	Gratefully yours	❑

3 Fill in the boxes with the correct word:

A formal letter should have your address at the top a) _____
hand side of the paper with the b) _____ directly beneath.
The company's address should appear on the left hand side on the same
level as the c) _____ .

4 Match with arrows which greeting goes with which ending:

Dear Sir
Dear Madam   Yours sincerely   Dear Sir/Madam
Dear Mr Thomas   Yours faithfully   Dear Ms Graham
                                     Dear Editor

5 Fill in the boxes with the correct word:

Diaries must include the a) _____ of the entry at the top of
the page and need not be written in complete b) _____
sentences.

✔ *If you got them all right, skip to page 45*

Special reports

Improve your knowledge

20 minutes

1 Letters to friends should have your address at the top right hand corner. Remember to include the date. Start the letter with Dear _____ .

2 The language should be kept lively, interesting and informal. Try to bear in mind who you are writing to and, therefore, whether the content of what you are writing is appropriate. Having just been to the end of term school party, a letter describing the event to your uncle in Scotland might be very different from a letter written to your best friend. At the end, it's a good idea to include a friendly farewell phrase.

3 Formal letters have your address in the top right hand corner with the date directly below. The address of the person you are writing to should be inserted at the left hand side, starting on the same level as the date.

Informal	Formal
Your address ············· ············· ··········· Date	Your address ············· ············· ········· Date
Dear···········	Their address ···················· ····················
	Dear···········
Best wishes ···················	Yours sincerely / faithfully ····················

43

4 The start and end of the letter must match. If you don't know the person's name, start the letter "Dear Sir" or "Dear Madam". If you don't know their gender, use "Dear Sir or Madam". End this type of letter with "Yours faithfully". If you know their name, you can start with "Dear Mr Thomas" and end with "Yours sincerely".

5 Diary entries need not be written in full grammatical sentences. Their function is to report the details of a day's activities, so they often contain both facts and some of the feelings and emotions of the writer. Don't forget to include the date at the top of each day.

Now learn how to use this knowledge

Special reports

Use your knowledge

20 minutes

1 Write a letter to your local newspaper explaining the changes and problems in your town.

Hint 1

■ Although there are plenty of street lamps, most of them don't work.

Hint 2

■ The one-way traffic system in your street has vastly improved the congestion problems.

Hint 3

■ Your elderly next door neighbour refuses to go out and you have had to go shopping for her for the last three weeks.

■ A group of youths who have recently moved to the area have started threatening old people and children in the streets in the evening.

■ All the teenagers who used to go to the local youth centre have left because a new group has taken over the club.

■ One boy at school has told you that this group of youths took all his money in an attack at night and said they would hurt him if he told anyone.

■ The litter bins in the centre of town are not being emptied daily.

Hint 4

■ There do not seem to be any police around the area at night.

Hint 5

_____

_____

_____

_____

_____

_____

_____ *(you may need to use more space)*

Hints and answers follow

Special reports

1   Think about the format you are going to use. You will need to find the full address of the Editor of your local paper. If you possibly can, always try to find out the name of the person to whom you are writing – it shows that you mean business and have put effort into your letter-writing!

2   Before planning what you want to write, select the information you want to write about. Discard anything that is not directly related to your points or argument, however interesting it might seem to be!

3   Remember to organise your argument: use the first paragraph to set out the reasons why you're writing.

4   Can you offer any suggestions to help solve the problems you're writing about? These should feature after your description of the problems themselves.

5   Show that you can present a balanced and reasonable argument by acknowledging the wider picture: in this case, can you comment on some of the reasons why the town's services are so run down in the first place?

1 Although your letter will be individual, use this model to check that you've included all the details in the correct format.

The Editor's address at the newspaper.	The date underneath your address.	Your address in the top right hand corner.

24 Rathbone Place
Humley
East Ridge
Bumpton
BU7 3ER.

3 April 1998

The Editor
East Ridge Chronicle
East Ridge
Bumpton
BU7 2WS.

The Editor's name is unknown, so an open greeting is needed.

Dear Sir/Madam,

States the problem, giving your examples as proof of the situation.

I am deeply disturbed by the presence of a gang of youths who have recently moved to East Ridge. They have been threatening both old people and children, particularly in the evening. My elderly next door neighbour is too frightened to go out any more and I have to do all her shopping for her. One boy at my school had his money stolen in an attack at night, but because he was threatened with physical violence if he told anyone, he has not reported the incident. As if all this was not enough, the gang have also taken over the youth club and now I have nowhere to meet up with my friends.

States reasons why the problems continue to exist.

One of the factors which allows these youths to behave in such a way is that a large number of the street lights in the town do not work and, therefore, in the darkened roads people are vulnerable to attack. I have not seen any police patrolling the area either, which means that the youths can behave just as they like.

Suggests a solution to solve the problems.

I do realise that budgets are tight, but surely we can spend some money on mending the street lamps and having a police presence on the streets at night. I think that both of these factors would help control these youths. It would certainly be better to have our town back the way it was.

The closing farewell must match the opening greeting.

Yours faithfully,

Mandy Sandwell

Mandy Sandwell

47

Reading narratives: plot

This chapter tests what you know and understand about the importance of plot in narrative. In your exam, you will be presented with a short story or extract from a novel and will have to answer questions on it. The examiners are looking for an ability to understand:

a) the importance of plot structure (this chapter)

b) the way characters are created (chapter on characters, page 55)

c) the way authors use settings (chapter on setting, page 63).

1 The word describing the main action of a narrative is the _____ .

2 The theme is the _____ .

3 The purpose of the beginning of a narrative is to _____

_____ .

4 The middle section is where the writer _____ themes.

5 An author uses expectation in a narrative to _____

_____ .

6 The _____ will normally resolve the issues that are raised in the narrative.

Answers

involve the reader **6** conclusion
5 create suspense, retain the reader's interest,
continue with the narrative **4** develops
3 interest the reader and encourage them to
1 plot **2** general idea of the narrative

✓ *If you got them all right, skip to page 50*

Reading narratives: plot

Improve your knowledge

20 minutes

1 Plot
This means the main events in the narrative. You can get the gist of it by reading over the narrative quickly, and by noting the characters' names and their relationships.

2 Theme
This is the main idea developed by the narrative. You will find that there are common themes that writers discuss and which appear throughout different kinds of literature. These include love, relationships, personal change, conflict and discovery.

3 Introduction
The first part of the narrative, which presents the themes and enables the writer to grab your attention.

4 Middle
The main body of the narrative, where the writer develops the themes or characters and issues raised in the introduction. There may be a twist where what you expected to happen does not: this creates surprise and dramatic tension.

5 Structure / narrative
This refers to the way the writer organises the narrative. There are a variety of narrative structures. Remember, the purpose of a narrative is to create interest. There are various techniques, such as expectation, that an author will use to make sure you keep reading right up until the end of the narrative.

6 Conclusion
This is the final part of the narrative. It should resolve some of the issues raised and provide you with relief! You will discover the effects of the characters' actions. The end of the narrative may not give you the answers to all your questions because it is sometimes more effective to keep you guessing.

Read the following passage adapted from *The Last Enemy,* by Richard Hillary, and answer the questions that follow:

I KNEW THAT MORNING that I was to kill for the first time. That I might be killed or in any way injured did not occur to me.

Later, when we were losing pilots regularly, I did consider it in an abstract way when on the ground, but once in the air, never. I knew it could not happen to me. I suppose every pilot knows that, knows it cannot happen to him; even when he is taking off for the last time, when he will not return, he knows that he cannot be killed. I wondered, idly, what he was like, this man I would kill. Was he young, was he handsome, would he die with the Führer's name on his lips, or would he die alone, in that last moment conscious of himself as a man? I would never know. Then I was being strapped in, my mind automatically checking the controls, and we were off.

We ran into them at 18,000 feet, twenty yellow-nosed Messerschmitt 109s, about 500 feet above us. Our Squadron strength was eight, and as they came down on us we went into line astern and turned head on to them. Brian Carbury, who was leading the Section, dropped the nose of his machine, and I could almost feel the leading Nazi pilot push forward on his stick to bring the guns to bear. At the same moment Brian hauled hard back on his own control stick and led us over them in a steep climbing turn to the left. In two vital seconds they lost their advantage. I saw Brian let go a burst of fire at the leading plane, saw the pilot put his machine into a half roll, and knew that he was mine. Automatically, I kicked the rudder to the left to get him at right angles, turned the gunbutton to "Fire", and let go in a four-second burst with full deflection. He came right through my sights and I saw the tracer from all eight guns thud home. For a second he seemed to hang motionless; then a jet of red flame shot upwards and he spun out of sight.

For the next few minutes I was too busy looking after myself to think of anything, but when, after a short while, they turned and made off over the Channel, and we were ordered to our base, my mind began to work again.

It had happened.

My first emotion was one of satisfaction, satisfaction at a job adequately done, at the final logical conclusion of months of specialised training. Then

I had a feeling of the essential rightness of it all. He was dead and I was alive; it could so easily have been the other way round. That would somehow have been right too. I realised in that moment just how lucky a fighter pilot is. He has none of the personalised emotions of the soldier, handed a rifle and bayonet and told to charge. He does not even have to share the dangerous emotions of the bomber pilot who, night after night, must experience that childish longing for smashing things. The fighter pilot's emotions are those of the duellist – cool, precise, impersonal. He is privileged to kill well. For if one must either kill or be killed, as now one must, it should, I feel, be done with dignity. Death should be given the setting it deserves. It should never be a pettiness; and for the fighter pilot it never can be.

1 Summarise the plot in five short statements.

Hint 1

a) _____

b) _____

c) _____

d) _____

e) _____

2 The theme of this narrative is _____ .

Hint 2

3 The introduction captures the reader's attention with the sentence a) " _____ " which is effective and grabs your attention because b) _____

Hint 3

_____ .

4 In the middle two paragraphs, the writer a) _____ the questions raised in the first paragraph and you know for certain that the character is not a b) _____ but a fighter pilot acting out of necessity.

Hint 4

5 The purpose of the conclusion is to _____

Hint 5

_____ .

51

6 The author uses expectation in this narrative at the

a) _____ because b) _____

_____ .

Hint 6

7 I considered the writing to be most effective when

a) _____ because b) _____ . The writer

achieves this by c) _____

_____ .

Hint 7

Reading narratives: plot

Hints

1   Take one point from each of the four main paragraphs and sum up the action. This will ensure that you understand the main action and can identify the important points.

2   Think about the overall ideas presented in the narrative. Usually, there will be just one main one.

3   What encourages you to continue reading? Look for the best quotation in the first paragraph to show this and comment on the impact it has on the reader.

4   Consider what the middle of this narrative contains and how it relates to the first paragraph. What did you think of the character when you read the first sentence of the narrative? Now what is your view of him?

5   Think about what the conclusion achieves and how it relates to the rest of the story.

6   Read the first paragraph again, and think about when you expect something to happen and what you expect to happen.

7   Remember to give a reason for why you found something effective and then say how the author achieves that effect. Practise giving your personal response and choose your words to describe it really carefully.

Reading narratives: plot

Answers

1. a) The narrator informs the reader that he is going to kill someone and describes how he will never know who the man was.
   b) Dramatic action between the English and Nazi squadrons when the narrator shoots a Nazi plane down.
   c) The narrator tells us that, for a short while, he cannot reflect on what he has done.
   d) The narrator tells us he has begun to think of what had happened after the attack.
   e) The narrator's view is that the fighter pilot's job is to kill and that it should be done well.

2. War and conflict. A sophisticated answer may include the personal dilemma of the narrator.

3. a) "I knew that morning that I was to kill for the first time."
   b) it is so horrific and is stated so clearly.

4. a) develops
   b) villain or murderer.

5. answer the doubts the narrator initially had, in the introduction, about killing someone.

6. a) beginning
   b) you expect the narrator to actually kill someone.

7. This requires a personal response and these are suggested answers:
   a) The narrator described the fight in the air
   b) it was dramatic and very vivid
   c) creating a sequence of sentences with lots of lively verbs and well-chosen adjectives in them.

Reading narratives: characters

10 minutes

In your exam, you will be asked to write about one or more of the characters from an extract. The most important points you'll need to think about are:

a) what features to look for when analysing characters

b) the importance of the words used to describe the characters

c) how to write about your personal response to characters.

1 Characters are _____ by an author.

Read the following passage from *Of Mice and Men*, by John Steinbeck, and answer the questions below:

> They had walked in single file down the path, and even in the open one stayed behind the other. Both were dressed in denim trousers and in denim coats with brass buttons. Both wore black, shapeless hats and both carried tight blanket rolls slung over their shoulders. The first man was small and quick, dark of face, with restless eyes and sharp, strong features. Every part of him was defined; small strong hands, slender arms, a thin and bony nose. Behind him walked his opposite, a huge man, shapeless of face, with large, pale eyes, with wide, sloping shoulders; and he walked heavily, dragging his feet a little, the way a bear drags his paws. His arms did not swing at his sides, but hung loosely and only moved because the heavy hands were pendula.

2 We gain important information about the characters through the way they are a) _____ . This tells us that these men b) _____ of a professional background.

3 The author describes the characters' _____ .

4 The two characters are opposites in the way they look. This is an effective technique because it makes us _____ them more.

5 The author portrays character through careful and deliberate use of _____ . The author is able to hide or _____ aspects of character. The author can _____ your opinion or view about the characters.

6 The examiners are looking for an a) _____ of how the author creates the character. You can achieve this by looking closely at the b) _____ the author uses to portray them.

7 The examiners are looking for your _____ response to the characters.

8 When writing about characters, you need to use three key things:
a) a _____ about the character
b) a _____ about the character
c) a _____ showing how the writer uses language to create an effective picture of the character.

If you got them all right, skip to page 59

Reading narratives: characters

20 minutes

1 Characters are not real people. However real they may seem, you should always remember that it is the writer who has created the character. Your task is to explain **how** the author presents the character.

2 Characters are presented through:

a) their behaviour, feelings and relationships, and the behaviour of others towards them

b) the language the author uses to inform you of this

c) what they wear

d) the setting they are depicted in.

3 An easy way to remember how to analyse character is to look at:

a) **what** the character does (speech, actions, thoughts)

b) **where** the character does it (setting, environment)   *Learn this*

c) **when** the character does it (plot structure)

d) **why** the character does it (motivations, plot structure)

e) **how** the character feels about what they have done (emotions, feelings).

4 The choice of words is very important because it gives you clues about the character. The author chooses the metaphor "the way a bear drags its paws" to describe Lennie's way of walking, revealing his size to you. It also hints to you of his nature; he has a gentle side but also physical strength. It is this which leads to an accidental murder later on in the book.

5 The author controls how you perceive characters and will choose to reveal things about their personalities at key points in the narrative. When they inform you of something this may alter your previous thoughts and opinions on the character. Make sure that you know your response to the character and notice when this changes, and why.

6 When writing about your response to a character, remember to include:

a) **what** you disliked/liked/found interesting about the character

b) **when** and **where** you discovered this in the text

c) **why** you came to this opinion of the character.

Learn this

7 Useful starting phrases to improve your discussion of characters could include:

I discovered, I thought, I interpreted, My opinion is, My feelings are, My analysis is, My understanding of, My assessment of, I considered, My response, and Personally, I felt.

Learn this

8 When you are writing about characters you must always use evidence from the text to support your statement. Think about it as if you are a lawyer in court:

a) **make a statement** about what you have learnt about the character

b) **provide your evidence** by using a reference to an event or a quotation

c) **comment on the words** the writer uses to describe the character.

Learn this

✔ *Now learn how to use this knowledge*

Reading narratives: characters

Use your knowledge

20 minutes

Read the following passage, adapted from *Of Mice and Men* by John Steinbeck. This is the first time that Lennie and George meet Curley's wife.

Answer the questions below after you've read this through twice.

> Both men glanced up, for the rectangle of sunshine in the doorway was cut off. A girl was standing there looking in. She had full, rouged lips and wide-spaced eyes, heavily made-up. Her fingernails were red. Her hair hung in little rolled clusters, like sausages. She wore a cotton house dress and red mules, on the insteps of which were little bouquets of red ostrich feathers. "I'm looking for Curley," she said. Her voice had a nasal, brittle quality.
>
> George looked away from her and then back. "He was in here a minute ago, but he went."
>
> "Oh!" She put her hands behind her back and leaned against the doorframe so that her body was thrown forward. "You're the new fellas that just come, ain't ya?"
>
> "Yeah."
>
> Lennie's eyes moved down over her body, and although she did not seem to be looking at Lennie, she bridled a little. She looked down at her fingernails. "Sometimes Curley's in here," she explained.
>
> George said brusquely, "Well, he ain't now."
>
> "If he ain't, I guess I better look someplace else," she said playfully.
>
> Lennie watched her, fascinated. George said, "If I see him, I'll pass word you was looking for him."
>
> She smiled archly and twitched her body. "Nobody can blame a person for lookin'," she said.

1 Steinbeck's description of the girl tells me that she is
a) _____ , b) _____ and c) _____ about (**Hint 1**)
her appearance. The repetition of the word d) _____
suggests to the reader that she is vivacious.

2 The narrative informs the reader that _____ and this supports Steinbeck's description of her physical appearance.

Hint 2

3 The way the girl acts emphasises her a) _____ attitude. This is evident from the quotation which describes the way she moves: b) " _____

_____ ."

Hint 3

4 A quotation to describe how Lennie responds to the girl is:

a) " _____ ."
The use of the word "fascinated" reveals the b) _____ the girl has on Lennie.

Hint 4

5 George's response to her is a) _____ to Lennie's response. We know this because the author reveals how George spoke to her: b) " _____ ". This dismissive roughness shows that he does not want to spend much time talking to her, and has a low opinion of her.

Hint 5

6 The author creates the character through a physical description which emphasises her make-up and _____ .

Hint 6

7 My view of this character is that she a) _____ .
The author achieves this by b) _____ .

Hint 7

8 The author reveals to us _____ .

Hint 8

Hints and answers to follow

Reading narratives: characters

Hints

1 Think about the overall features of the girl's character.

2 Does her speech support your initial thoughts of her character?

3 How does she approach the ranch men? What actions support this view?

4 Remember how you learn about the character from the way that others respond to her. What does Lennie's reaction tell us about his feelings towards her?

5 There are sometimes a variety of views about a character from other characters. This helps the reader gain an all-round view. Look at the words Steinbeck chooses to describe the way George speaks to her.

6 Certain aspects of a character are always more evident than others: these may be more important. What does Steinbeck repeat, in various ways, about the girl?

7 Your personal response is vital. Remember, you may have a different view from those of your friends. This is always a good thing, provided you can support and explain your views.

8 What is the main thing the author reveals to us about the girl's character?

Reading narratives: characters

Answers

1 a) trying to get attention b) flirtatious c) cares a lot d) red.

2 she is a flirt

3 a) teasing b) "She put her hands behind her back and leaned against the door frame so that her body was thrown forward."

4 "Lennie watched her, fascinated." b) dramatic effect

5 a) different b) "brusquely"

6 appearance

7 a) is looking for attention/is a flirt/is a tease/feels lonely and wants some company b) describing, in detail, her appearance, behaviour and the responses of other characters to her.

8 how the girl has different effects on the male characters and that Lennie is very taken by her.

Reading narratives: setting

10 minutes

The examiners are interested in how well you explain the importance of setting to the narrative. The most important points to consider are:

a) what the setting adds to the story

b) what to look for

c) how to write about setting.

1 The setting of a narrative is the _____ .

2 One purpose of the setting is to make the _____ more descriptive.

3 A setting helps to _____ .

4 Examples of different types of setting an author may use are
a) _____ , b) _____ and c) _____ .

5 The setting of the narrative can give us valuable information about the _____ in the story.

6 The setting will also be important in helping us to identify and understand the _____ and emotions of the characters.

7 In describing the setting, the author will use _____ language to make the scene vivid for the reader.

✓ *If you got them all right, skip to page 66*

Reading narratives: setting

Improve your knowledge

20 minutes

1 A story will obviously always take place somewhere; it can be an actual place, country, city or rural area. It can be as bizarre as space, a different planet or even a different period in history.

2 An author will bring to life the setting of his or her story by using descriptive prose. Your task is to think about

  a) what that setting is

  b) how the setting contributes to the story

  c) how the writer uses language to create the setting.

Learn this

3 A good use of setting will enable the reader to experience the world of the narrative as the character actually sees it. This helps the reader to understand the characters' thoughts, actions and feelings. Always write about setting alongside what you know about the plot and character.

4 There are a variety of **types** of setting. Common ones include:

  a) idyllic, rural, natural, country landscapes

  b) urban, man-made, industrial, city

  c) wild areas, exposed to the harsh weather and sparsely inhabited

  d) rough raging seascapes.

5 The type of setting the author chooses helps the reader to appreciate the theme of the story. For example: Emily Brontë uses wild, untamed Yorkshire moors for the setting of the passionate, violent and ghostly love story of Heathcliff and Cathy in *Wuthering Heights*.

6 The way the author chooses to describe the weather, in particular, helps the reader to gain an understanding of the mood of the characters. For example, a storm is a good setting for a character who is feeling enraged. Think about how film directors often use thunder in horror movies when something frightening or unpleasant is about to happen. It all adds to the atmosphere!

Another way of using setting is to make it **contrast** with the mood of the character. For instance, a description of a beautiful sunny day when a character is very upset can make you have more sympathy for the character's feelings.

7 The author can bring words to life using well chosen descriptive language. You have to use your imagination to allow the words to work on you. A useful way of doing this is to use your five senses:

a) **See** the colours. Do they contrast or harmonise and is this relevant to the plot?

b) **Hear** the sounds. Are they loud, monotonous or musical and how does this relate to the atmosphere that is created?

Learn this

c) **Taste** the flavours. Are they sharp, sweet, bitter, or tangy? How does this relate to the plot?

d) **Feel** the sensations described, including hot, cold, biting, stuffy and invigorating. How do these relate to the characters' emotions?

e) **Smell** the aromas. Are they fresh and pungent, or reeking? How does the smell being described contribute to the narrative?

You may only find one or two of a) – e) in your narrative but it is important that you **notice** them and **apply** what you have noticed to the rest of the text.

Now learn how to use this knowledge

Reading narratives: setting

Use your knowledge

Read the following passage adapted from *As I Walked Out One Midsummer Morning* by Laurie Lee, and answer the questions that follow.

> I was nineteen years old, still soft at the edges, but with a confident belief in good fortune. I carried a small rolled-up tent, a violin in a blanket, a change of clothes and a tin of treacle biscuits. I was excited, vain-glorious, knowing I had far to go: but not as yet, how far. As I left home that morning and walked away from the sleeping village, it never occurred to me that others had done this before me.
>
> I was propelled, of course, by the traditional forces that had sent many generations along this road – by the small tight valley closing in around one, stifling the breath with its mossy mouth, the cottage walls narrowing like the arms of an iron maiden, the local girls whispering, "Marry, and settle down." Months of restless unease, leading to this inevitable moment, had been spent wandering about the hills, mournfully whistling, and watching the high open fields stepping away eastwards under gigantic clouds…

1 The type of setting Laurie Lee creates here is _____ . **Hint 1**

2 The use of this type of setting is effective in suggesting character because _____ **Hint 2**
_____ .

3 The author uses _____ in lines 2 and 3 to encourage the reader to think about the peculiar items the narrator carries on his journey. **Hint 3**

4 The use of the a) _____ in lines 7–9 is to portray to the reader b) _____ . **Hint 4**

5 The use of the _____ in line 10 emphasises the restrictions the narrator has felt while living in the village.

Hint 5

6 A suitable quotation to describe the narrator's interaction with the setting would be " _____ ".

Hint 6

7 The last phrase, "gigantic clouds", gives me the impression that the narrator feels _____ .

Hint 7

Hints and answers follow

Reading narratives: setting

1   Think about where the narrative is set and what the characteristics of the setting are.

2   Look at the plot and then at the setting. Why do they go together well? How does one support the other?

3   A device to allow the author to put lots of items in the same sentence.

4   The author uses metaphorical language here. It is good to get the reader to think of comparisons and similarities to other things to help them visualise scenes. Think about how the narrator feels the village has limited his options. Look for a metaphor that describes this.

5   Look for a literary device that helps the reader appreciate further the way the narrator feels about how he has a lack of opportunities to explore.

6   Look for a suitable quotation to summarise the narrator's interaction with the setting. It tells us that he had been restless and impatient to escape the countryside.

7   You have to imagine what it must be like for the narrator. Use your senses to really place yourself in his shoes. What must those gigantic clouds mean to him?

Reading narratives: setting

Answers

1 an idyllic, rural, peaceful, countryside setting

2 the narrator describes himself as having an innocent outlook on life. He is also pure and natural, like the setting

3 listing

4 a) metaphor b) the limitations of the environment

5 simile

6 "Months of restless unease, leading to this inevitable moment, had been spent wandering about the hills, mournfully whistling"...

7 that there is something more exciting waiting to be explored outside his childhood village.

Writing narratives

10 minutes

Test your knowledge

In your exam you will be asked to write a narrative in response to what you have read. Answer these questions to see if you know what the examiners are looking for in your answers.

1 Examiners are looking to see how well I can organise my
a) _____ . The best way of making sure the structure of my work is clear is to b) _____ before I begin my essay.

2 The purpose of my narrative is to write the story in a
a) _____ way and to b) _____ the reader.

3 The three important areas I need to think about when I am writing a narrative are a) _____ , b) _____ and
c) _____ .

4 When I am thinking about the plot of my story I need to make it
_____ so that the reader does not think what happens is impossible.

5 When I am creating characters in the narrative I will be describing
a) _____ , b) _____ , c) _____ and
d) _____ .

6 To make my story more effective I will need to think about the setting of the narrative. To do this I will be describing _____ .

Answers

1 a) ideas b) plan my work 2 a) personal
b) engage or interest 3 a) plot b) character
c) setting 4 believable 5 a) what they say
b) what they do c) what they look like d) how
others respond to them 6 the environment
the characters are in

If you got them all right, skip to page 73

1 Structure and essay planning

Examiners are looking for organised essays. To make sure you do your ideas justice, always write an essay plan. Spend ten minutes making notes before you start your essay and you will improve your grade. Don't panic just because everyone else seems to have written a page! If they haven't planned properly, they will no doubt run out of ideas or forget what they wanted to write anyway. Take your time and invest in a well thought-out plan.

2 Writing for an audience

Remember that someone will be reading your work. Try to make your story interesting by thinking carefully about their response. Check your language is appropriate for your purpose. Be descriptive and entertaining by using your five senses to really bring your story to life. This will help to draw the reader into the world of your story.

Avoid repeating "I said", "She said", "Then I said"! Add a bit of interesting detail. Alternatives might be "screamed", "replied", "commanded", "cheered", "explained" or "revealed".

Try to avoid repeating "did". Try "suddenly", "without warning", "I continued to…" and so on.

3 Planning your essay

Plan your essay with three things in mind:

a) **plot:** what happens in the narrative?
   Make sure you know how your story develops and how it will end before you begin to write.

b) **character:** who is in your narrative?
   Avoid having more than two main characters, otherwise it can get very complicated. Just concentrate on carefully revealing one or two for maximum effect.

c) **setting:** what is the environment in which your characters are set? This helps the reader to picture your story and makes it much more interesting.

4 Realism

Make sure that your plots are imaginative but believable. The ending where a character wakes up to find it has all been a dream is probably the most used and least interesting ending ever! When you plan your essay have four or five main events that occur, one in each paragraph.

5 Character

For successful character creations think about:

a) **what they look like**, eg. are they tall, short, friendly-looking?

b) **what they do and how they do it**, eg. do they walk with a limp, are they forgetful or always late?

c) **what they say and how they say it**, eg. do they speak angrily, calmly, or with heightened emotion? *Learn this*

d) **how other characters respond to them**, eg. is your character popular or lonely?

6 Setting

Try to make the environment of the character come to life for your reader. Think about the following points:

a) what does your setting **look like**? *Learn this*

b) are there particular **sounds**?

c) what does it **feel like** for the character to be in that environment?

Now learn how to use this knowledge

Writing narratives

Use your knowledge

Imagine you have just read a story about a young boy who describes his feelings the night before his first day at a new senior school. You are now asked to write, as if you were the boy, about what happens the next day at school.

1 The question is asking me to _____ .

Hint 1

2 The story will be quite personal because I will be writing in the _____ .

Hint 2

3 The major things that will happen in my story are :

a) _____

b) _____

c) _____

Hint 3

d) _____

e) _____

4 My character has the following key features:

a) physical _____ .

b) action _____ .

c) speech _____ .

Hint 4

d) other characters' responses to him or her _____ .

5 Descriptions of each of the places in my story are as follows :

Hint 5

a) _____

b) _____

c) _____

6 Additional details:

Hint 6

a) _____

_____

_____

_____

_____

b) _____

_____

_____

_____

_____

c) _____

_____

_____

_____

_____

_____

Hints and answers follow

Writing narratives

Hints

1 Remember to break down the question first. Think about what the character is likely to be feeling.

2 From whose point of view are you being asked to write?

3 Think of the main things that will happen in your story. Say something about what will happen about each of these things. Allow an equal amount of time for each to help ensure that you won't run out of time. Try to make it different or unusual.

4 Sometimes it helps to use features of people you actually know to make your character realistic: this is a great way to develop characters if you are really stuck for ideas!

5 Use your own experience of school to help you with making the school setting more interesting and realistic for the reader.

6 Obviously, this is individual. Can you think of original ways of weaving character, setting and plot together? Remember, each event needs to relate to the previous one in some way. Ensure you don't spend too long on the first paragraph, then run out of time and have to end the story very abruptly and awkwardly.

Writing narratives

Answers

Remember, these are **suggested** answers. Your ideas will be different but should be interesting to read.

1 consider the events and feelings involved in a boy's first day at senior school

2 first person

3 Plot:
  a) Late bus: bus broke down, needed to catch second bus
  b) Assembly: sneezing attack, very embarrassing
  c) Maths lesson: got all the sums correct but got homework anyway
  d) Dinner: forgot sandwiches, had to use bus fare to buy lunch
  e) Physics: did not understand anything, mad science teacher.

4 Character:
  a) Appearance: hair that always sticks up, no matter what he does to it, and freckles.
  b) Walks with his feet turned out and nickname is Duckling. He's always late for everything.
  c) Is quite cheeky when he speaks to teachers.
  d) Is popular because he's funny and makes the others laugh.

5 Setting:
  a) Bus: empty because it's after 9 am: makes the character more anxious.
  b) School: bigger than expected, tall, forbidding, even the windows look scary.
  c) Assembly: smells of disinfectant and the mustiness of years of bored schoolchildren.

6 Additional details: a) Dinner: looks like a cattle market, smells of putrid cabbage, custard was pink and lumpy. b) Physics: teacher looked like someone out of *Jurassic Park*, mad scientist with a glint in his left eye. Lots of wires, lights and crocodile clips. Clipped one to his jacket, rest of the class laughed. c) Home: walk home took an hour, brighter than this morning. Walked across the park for a shortcut, saw the mad scientist on way home.

Understanding poetry

Test your knowledge

10 minutes

Read the following poem, *Anthem for Doomed Youth* by Wilfred Owen, and answer the questions about it below.

In each question the initial letter of the missing word is given.

What passing-bells for these who die as cattle?
    Only the monstrous anger of the guns.
    Only the stuttering rifles' rapid rattle
Can patter out their hasty orisons.
No mockeries now for them; no prayers nor bells,
    Nor any voice of mourning save the choirs,
The shrill, demented choirs of wailing shells;
      And bugles calling for them from sad shires.

What candles may be held to speed them all?
    Not in the hands of boys, but in their eyes
Shall shine the holy glimmers of good-byes.
    The pallor of girls' brows shall be their pall;
Their flowers the tenderness of patient minds,
And each slow dusk a drawing-down of blinds.

1 The s_____ of the poem is often suggested by the title.

2 In reading a poem you will quickly understand its m_____ .
This is a way of describing the structure and style of a poem.

3 A poem can have different types of i_____ to the help the
reader picture (or even smell or feel) what is going on.

4 The l_____ used in a poem should not always be taken literally;
but it is important to see how a writer chooses and uses words.

5 The e_____ evoked by the poem will given an indication of the poet's view of the subject.

6 A poet will have his or her views but your r_____ is equally important.

7 Reading a poem aloud and listening to its s_____ is another good way of understanding what the writer is wishing to say.

✓ *If you got them all right, skip to page 81*

Understanding poetry

Improve your knowledge

20 minutes

An explanation of the answers 1–7 is given on page 80, but before you read this, consider **smilers** – a good way of understanding and explaining a poem. The **smilers** technique asks you to think about **subject, movement, imagery, language, emotion, response** and **sound**.

Smilers	Definition	Hints	Alternative words
Subject	This is what the poem is about.	Look at the **title** or at words in the poem which are about the same thing.	Theme, ideas, topic., thoughts.
Movement	This describes what ideas come first and how they **develop**.	Does each verse begin or end with a similar idea? Do the ideas change by the time you get to the end of the poem?	Structure, organisation
Imagery	This is when the poet makes you use your **imagination** by using words which make the reader see things or hear things. Sometimes you can almost taste, feel or touch things.	Use your imagination and your five senses when you read poetry.	Pictures, symbols
Language	The words a writer **chooses** and **how** they are put together.	Think imaginatively, not always literally. Remember, just because a poem has the word "cattle" in does not mean it is a poem about cows. A poet may also use **metaphors** and **similes** to make his or her ideas known.	Diction, expression
Emotion	The feelings the speaker has in the poem.	You have to **listen** here and you will pick up the **tone**. does your teacher say "be quiet" in the same way all the time or can you sense how they are feeling from the way they say it?	Feelings, thoughts, opinions, attitudes.
Response	Your thoughts about the poem.	Don't be shy, examiners often like to know you have some thoughts about what you read. **Be specific** and say what you liked and why.	Surprising, unusual, difficult, thought-provoking, stirring, upsetting, consoling, amusing.
Sound	The way the words sound often gives you more information about what the poem is about.	Read the poem aloud or in your head.. Note words which made you think of their sound and go back to them later.	I hear, it sounds like, it reminds me of.

Here is *Anthem For Doomed Youth*, annotated with the **smilers** method. Note that the examples of metaphor, simile, imagery and personification from question 7 are also explained.

What passing-bells for these who die as cattle? ◄——— **subject**
Only the monstrous anger of the guns.
Only the stuttering rifles' rapid rattle ◄——————— **sound**
Can patter out their hasty orisons.
No mockeries now for them; no prayers nor bells, ◄— **movement**
Nor any voice of mourning save the choirs,
The shrill, demented choirs of wailing shells;
And bugles calling for them from sad shires. ◄——— **emotion**

What candles may be held to speed them all?
Not in the hands of boys, but in their eyes
Shall shine the holy glimmers of good-byes.
The pallor of girls' brows shall be their pall;
imagery ➙ Their flowers the tenderness of patient minds,
And each slow dusk a drawing-down of blinds. ◄——— **language**

1 **Subject:** what the poem is about. In this case, young soldiers.

2 **Movement:** notice how the poet answers the question here. The soldiers will not have prayers, bells or voices to guide them from life to death.

3 **Imagery:** flowers are delicate and this is a metaphor for the sadness of the death of the soldiers.

4 **Language:** the closing of the blinds is like the closing of the eyes of these dead men.

5 **Emotion:** the poem ends on a sad and sorrowful note as death approaches.

6 **Response:** I found this poem very moving, and was left asking why these men had to die in this way.

7 **Sound:** echoing repetitions of the rifles' noise. The word "monstrous" sounds hollow and low: this adds to the sombre mood of the poem.

Understanding poetry

Use your knowledge

Read Wilfred Owen's poem again. You will be using the **smilers** technique to answer the questions. There are hints on the next page to help you, and answers on page 83.

1 The subject of Wilfred Owen's poem is _____ .

Hint 1

2 The poem moves from asking a _____ in the first line of each verse to answering it in the rest of the verse.

Hint 2

3 Owen uses imagery to make the poem powerful. An image I thought was especially good was a) _____ because b) _____ .

Hint 3

4 One example of Owen's effective use of language is _____ .

Hint 4

5 The emotions expressed in this poem include _____ .

Hint 5

6 I found the poem _____ _____ .

Hint 6

7 An example of Owen's effective use of sound is _____ _____ .

Hint 7

Hints and answers follow

Understanding poetry

Hints

1. Look at the title. It gives you a hint about the subject of the poem. See if there are a lot of words about the same thing in the poem.

2. Look at the first line of the first verse again. What does it ask?

3. a) Remember, an image is when a word or phrase almost makes you hear, see, taste, touch or smell something. Try to use your imagination.

   b) You need to say why you thought the image was powerful.

4. Remember, poetry is a special way of using words and a poet has to choose each word carefully and economically.

5. Listen to the way the words sound. Try reading the first and last lines of every verse to give you a clue. There is usually more than one emotion in the poem: there may even be mixed emotions.

6. This is where you get to say how you felt about the poem. For the short amount of time you have read the poem you have been in another world, the world of dying young soldiers in the war. Perhaps you were absorbed in the way the girls feel. How did it feel to be in that world?

7. Read the poem again and underline words where you think the way they sound adds to the meaning of the poem. You will also notice how many words are to do with sound in this poem.

Understanding poetry

Answers

Your answer will be individual, but it should include something of the following:

1 young men dying in the war/the injustice of war/the awful way the young men died

2 question

3 a) "holy glimmers of good-byes"

   b) it made me think of the light of life going out in the men's eyes

4 "shrill, demented choirs of wailing shells"

5 anger/sadness/grief/sympathy/questioning/melancholy/frustration

6 moving/sad/sorrowful/painful/pitiful

7 "stuttering rifles' rapid rattle".

Mock exam

1 hour

1 Before your real GCSE examination you will be given plenty of time to read a short story before being tested on it. We suggest you take about 30 minutes to read the following short story from *Dubliners* by James Joyce. Then, perhaps an hour or two (or even a day) later, come back to this exam. This time allow yourself one hour to re-read the story and answer the question that follows.

Eveline

She sat at the window watching the evening invade the avenue. Her head was leaned against the window curtains, and in her nostrils was the odour of dusty cretonne. She was tired.

Few people passed. The man out of the last house passed on his way home; she heard his footsteps clacking along the concrete pavement and afterwards crunching on the cinder path before the new red houses. One time there used to be a field there in which they used to play every evening with other people's children. Then a man from Belfast bought the field and built houses in it – not like their little brown houses, but bright brick houses with shining roofs. The children of the avenue used to play together in that field – the Devines, the Waters, the Dunns, little Keogh the cripple, she and her brothers and sisters. Ernest, however, never played: he was too grown up. Her father used often to hunt them in out of the field with his blackthorn stick; but usually little Keogh used to keep nix and call out when he saw her father coming. Still they seemed to have been rather happy then. Her father was not so bad then; and besides, her mother was alive. That was a long time ago; she and her brothers and sisters were all grown up; her mother was dead. Tizzie Dunn was dead, too, and the Waters had gone back to England. Everything changes. Now she was going to go away like the others, to leave her home.

Home! She looked round the room, reviewing all its familiar objects which she had dusted once a week for so many years, wondering where on earth all the dust came from. Perhaps she would never see again those familiar objects from which she had never dreamed of being divided. And yet during all those years she had never found out the name of the priest whose yellowing photograph hung on the wall above the broken harmonium beside the coloured print of the promises made to Blessed Margaret Mary Alacoque. He had been a school friend of her father. Whenever he showed the photograph to a visitor her father used to pass it with a casual word:

"He is in Melbourne now."

She had consented to go away, to leave her home. Was that wise? She tried to weigh each side of the question. In her home anyway she had shelter and food; she had those whom she had known all her life about her. Of course she had to work hard, both in the house and at business. What would they say of her in the Stores when they found out that she had run away with a fellow? Say she was a fool, perhaps; and her place would be filled up by advertisement. Miss Gavan would be glad. She had always had an edge on her, especially whenever there were people listening.

"Miss Hill, don't you see these ladies are waiting?"

"Look lively, Miss Hill, please."

She would not cry many tears at leaving the Stores.

But in her new home, in a distant unknown country, it would not be like that. Then she would be married – she, Eveline. People would treat her with respect then. She would not be treated as her mother had been. Even now, though she was over nineteen, she sometimes felt herself in danger of her father's violence. She knew it was that that had given her the Palpitations. When they were growing up he had never gone for her, like he used to go for Harry and Ernest, because she was a girl; but latterly he had begun to threaten her and say what he would do to her only for her dead mother's sake. And now she had nobody to protect her, Ernest was dead and Harry, who was in the church decorating business, was nearly always down somewhere in the country. Besides, the invariable squabble for money on Saturday nights had begun to weary her unspeakably. She always gave her entire wages – seven shillings – and Harry always sent up what he could, but the trouble was to get any money from her father. He said she used to squander the money, that she had no head, that he wasn't going to give her his hard-earned money to throw about the streets, and much more, for he was usually fairly bad on Saturday night. In the end he would give her the money and ask her had she any intention of buying Sunday's dinner. Then she had to rush out as quickly as she could and do her marketing, holding her black leather purse tightly in her hand as she elbowed her way through the crowds and returning home late under her load of provisions. She had hard work to keep the house together and to see that the two young children who had been left to her charge went to school regularly and got their meals regularly. It was hard work – a hard life – but now that she was about to leave it she did not find it a wholly undesirable life.

She was about to explore another life with Frank. Frank was very kind, manly, open-hearted. She was to go away with him by the night-boat to be his wife and to live with him in Buenos Aires, where he had a home waiting for her. How well she remembered the first time she had seen him; he was lodging in a house on the main road where she used to visit. It seemed a few weeks ago. He was standing at the gate, his peaked cap pushed back on his head and his hair tumbled forward over a face of bronze. Then they had come to know each other. He used to meet her outside the Stores every evening and see her home. He took her to see 'The Bohemian Girl' and she felt elated as she sat in an unaccustomed part of the theatre with him. He was awfully fond of music and sang a little. People knew that they were courting and, when he sang about the lass that loves a sailor, she always felt pleasantly confused. He used to call her Poppens out of fun. First of all it had been an excitement for her to have a fellow and then she had begun to like him. He had tales of distant countries. He had started as a deck boy at a pound a month on a ship of the Allan Line going out to Canada. He told her the names of the ships he had been on and the names of the different services. He had sailed through the Straits of Magellan and he told her stories of the terrible Patagonians. He had fallen on his feet in Buenos Aires, he said, and had come over to the old country just for a holiday. Of course, her father had found out about the affair and had forbidden her to have anything to say to him.

"I know these sailor chaps" he said.

One day he had quarrelled with Frank, and after that she had to meet her lover secretly.

The evening deepened in the avenue. The white of two letters in her lap grew indistinct. One was to Harry; the other was to her father. Ernest had been her favourite, but she liked Harry too. Her father was becoming old lately, she noticed; he would miss her. Sometimes he could be very nice. Not long before, when she had been laid up for a day, he had read her out a ghost story and made toast for her at the fire. Another day, when their mother was alive, they had all gone for a picnic to the Hill of Howth. She remembered her father putting on her mother's bonnet to make the children laugh.

Her time was running out, but she continued to sit by the window, leaning her head against the window curtain, inhaling the odour of dusty cretonne. Down far in the avenue she could hear a street organ playing. She knew the air. Strange that it should come that very night to remind her of the promise to her mother, her promise to keep the home together as long as she could. She remembered the last night of her mother's illness; she was again in the close, dark room at the other side of the hall and outside she heard a melancholy air of Italy. The organ-player had been ordered to go away and given sixpence. She remembered her father strutting back into the sick-room saying:

"Damned Italians! coming over here!"

As she mused, the pitiful vision of her mother's life laid its spell on the very quick of her being – that life of commonplace sacrifices closing in final craziness. She trembled as she heard again her mother's voice saying constantly with foolish insistence:

"Derevaun Seraun! Derevaun Seraun!"

She stood up in a sudden impulse of terror. Escape! She must escape! Frank would save her. He would give her life, perhaps love, too. But she wanted to live. Why should she be unhappy? She had a right to happiness. Frank would take her in his arms, fold her in his arms. He would save her.

She stood among the swaying crowd in the station at the North Wall. He held her hand and she knew that he was speaking to her, saying something about the passage over and over again. The station was full of soldiers with brown baggages. Through the wide doors of the sheds she caught a glimpse of the black mass of the boat, lying in beside the quay wall, with illumined portholes. She answered nothing. She felt her cheek pale and cold and, out of a maze of distress, she prayed to God to direct her, to show her what was her duty. The boat blew a long mournful whistle into the mist. If she went, tomorrow she would be on the sea with Frank, steaming towards Buenos Aires. Their passage had been booked. Could she still draw back after all he had done for her? Her distress awoke a nausea in her body and she kept moving her lips in silent fervent prayer.

A bell clanged upon her heart. She felt him seize her hand: "Come!"

All the seas of the world tumbled about her heart. He was drawing her into them: he would drown her. She gripped with both hands at the iron railing.

"Come!"

No! No! No! It was impossible. Her hands clutched the iron in frenzy. Amid the seas she sent a cry of anguish.

"Eveline! Evvy!"

He rushed beyond the barrier and called to her to follow. He was shouted at to go on, but he still called to her. She set her white face to him, passive, like a helpless animal. Her eyes gave him no sign of love or farewell or recognition.

Note: Cretonne is a strong printed fabric used for curtains.

a) **Describe Eveline's feelings towards her home life and the life that she is considering with Frank.**

_____

_____

_____

_____

_____

_____

_____

_____

_____

_____

_____

_____

_____

_____

_____

_____

_____

_____

_____

_____

_____

_____

_____

_____

Mock exam hints

1   Always read the exam paper right through at the start. Don't be afraid that everyone will have already begun writing; they may not have read the instructions and are perhaps making mistakes. You will need to read the material really carefully before you answer each question. Take ten minutes to do this.

2 **The plot**

You will need to remember the following when you consider the plot:

a) Read the narrative quickly to get the gist of it.

b) Note the characters' names, relationships, etc.

Learn this

c) Read the question with care.

d) Read the text again, highlighting important parts.

You should notice the title of the short story: this is obviously going to be about a girl. You should realise, from the content of the story, that its themes are relationships and change.

3 **The characters**

Look at the way Joyce describes Eveline to you as a reader. We are told about various stages in her life; her childhood with her friends, her family, her present job, her father and what her future might be like with Frank. To help you, here are some extra hints:

a) **What the character does (plot)**

Eveline's thoughts are described to us through the narrator, so this is a **third person narrative**. The reader is given an insight into what Eveline feels throughout the story. Her feelings change from regret to fear about the prospect of leaving and fear about what her future will hold. She is also excited at having "status" as a married woman but then we are informed that she will miss her home because it is a place that provides shelter and security.

b) **Where the character does it (setting)**

Joyce sets the story in Eveline's home and uses lots of specific detail to describe her environment. The reader is able to see her home from her point of view and is then more able to sympathise with her.

c) **When the character does it (plot)**

Joyce keeps the reader in suspense because we do not know exactly what Eveline will do until the very end of the story and we are encouraged to think that she will go with Frank, whereas she does not. This keeps the reader interested in the story.

d) **Why the character does it (character)**

Think about the information that Joyce has given to you about Eveline's present life. Her fondness for her home is emphasised as is her longing for security and safety.

e) **How the character feels (character)**

It is clear at the end of the story that Eveline is terrified and is in shock by the way that Joyce describes her as gripping the iron railings. The reader knows that she is not happy about the fact that she does not go with Frank but it is as if the decision has been made for her to stay at home.

4 **The setting**

The setting enables the reader to experience the world of the narrative as the central character actually sees it. This helps the reader to understand the character's thoughts, actions and feelings. Remember to include information on the following:

a) **What the setting is**

The main setting in the story is Eveline's home. This is described in detail so the reader is able to see what life is like for Eveline.

b) **How the setting contributes to the story**

It is important to see what life is like for Eveline because the story is about whether she decides to leave her home or not. The reader has to understand what Eveline's home means to her.

c) **How the writer uses language to create the setting**

Joyce uses the senses of sight, sound and smell to create the setting. We see the man walking past the window as Eveline does and we hear his footsteps. We can almost smell the dusty curtains where Eveline is sitting. This is very effective because it introduces us to Eveline by describing what she sees, hears and smells. It makes us more likely to be sympathetic towards her.

Mock exam answer

First of all, look carefully at the question again.

a) Describe Eveline's feelings towards her home life and the life that she is considering with Frank.

Make sure that you understand every part of the question, including the following terms and phrases:

Describe: put in your own words.
Eveline's feelings: what are her thoughts, feelings, emotions.
Home life: her life with her father, her younger brothers and sisters, her feelings towards her mother, her childhood, her life at the Stores, and her home town.
Life with Frank: what her life as a wife to Frank in a different country means to her.

Now that you are entirely clear about what the question wants, you can plan your response. Here is a simple essay plan to help you with this:

Introduction

Eveline feels more than one thing about her home life and Frank. This makes the story interesting and realistic because Joyce has created a believable character who has lots of different, conflicting feelings.

Main points

1 **Home life.** We find out about the place where she grew up and that she feels nostalgic. The setting helps the reader to share her nostalgia.

2 **Home life.** We learn of her father's behaviour towards her and that she feels afraid.

3 **Home life.** She will not be missed at the Stores and will certainly not miss her job. She will have no regrets about leaving this.

4 **Frank.** She will have "status" and be considered an adult rather than a child if she marries. She will have her independence.

5 **Frank.** She will be saved and protected from the life her mother had with her father. She feels relief at this.

Conclusion

Summarise Eveline's feelings throughout the passage. Show that she is a realistic character who experiences a range of emotions about her situation. Include a personal response to her decision not to go with Frank at the end of the story: did you think she would go? How might you personally have responded?